Life of an

Unknown Lady

By

Chelock Mitchell

Prologue

In "Life of an Unknown Lady," Chelock Mitchell offers a tender and profound invitation into a life lived with an open heart and unyielding spirit. From echoes of a post-war childhood to the quiet reflective years of later life. She illustrates her personal story about hardship, strengthened faith, and joy of life in the most unexpected moments.

This book is more than a collection of memories; It offers a reflection on how faith, family and inner strength helped and endure to overcome many storms in her life. This story is truly reflecting the gain of wisdom through mistake and victory. It is all about the reality of life. Which not only depends on its meaning but also profound on its impact on every movement.

Dedication

This book is dedicated to my grand-daughter, Roslyn Murphy. You are the one in my life who always remains with me. From your childhood till now; your love and support have never wavered. You lived with me, laughed with me, and lifted me through more than you may ever realize. I am feeling a great honor to have you and your unexpected support. Dear Roslyn, your love and support is woven on every page of this book.

Acknowledgement

I would like to thank a classmate who stood beside me during the writing of this book. Your support and encouragement means a lot to me. Especially the memories you shared about your brother who was also an author.

To all my friends and the kind individuals whom I met in my whole life and those having a strong impact on my life.

I am also thankful to the classmates of my late son. Their kindness and generosity remained with me during hard time and for this I highly appreciated. You all stood by me during one of the hardest times. Offering comfort to me when I lose everything in my life.

Lastly, I thank my pastor, whom strength and faith touched many lives including mine. His prayers and healing ministry continues to inspire me.

To all those people who believed in me even in bad times of my life. I am thankful to all of you from the depths of my heart. And to my closest friends who quietly support me to articulate this story into a masterpiece.

Table of Contents

Chapter 1: Seeds of Small Beginnings

My name was Chelock. A name which rolled off people's tongues as they spoke it, usually stumbled into a mispronunciation. A name which singled me out, one whose etymology was unknown even to myself. I only ever knew frustration whenever anyone butchered it.

Chelock or something completely different. A minor annoyance in a larger context perhaps, but for a child, it was an affront in a society which highly values uniformity.

Life of an Unknown Lady

I was born on June 7, 1947, in a small house nestled in a secluded corner of the world recovering from scars inflicted by war. The house in which I was raised was small, but it was vibrant and alive with laughter sweeping through the clang of pots, the hum of voices, and the occasional groaning of old wooden floorboards.

We weren't wealthy in material possessions but rich in spirit, our days blessed by the sort of love and resilience that money can't buy happiness.

My childhood was a rich tapestry of simplicity and family warmth. Through its center stood my brother James, a soldier who returned every six months for a visit that was always the highlight of my childhood. James was bigger than life, with his booming laugh and heart as wide as the sky.

When James arrived home for a visit, he'd pick me up in his arms and call me his "little princess" and take me on adventures throughout the town. He had purchased candies, cookies, soda and whatever I wanted.

To James, I was incapable of doing anything wrong and he catered to every desire I had, making me a precious little girl who believed everything in the world had belonged to her.

That princess's treatment of my brother, how wonderful those moments had its positive sides. I learned that I could get what I wanted simply by smiling or throwing a tantrum. I would not even eat anything healthy, making faces at vegetables and pitching a fit about getting my teeth brushed because in my thinking James would always make it right.

My parents, bless them, tried to rein me in, but my doting brother made me bold and taught me an ability to manipulate circumstances and a knack that foreshadowed the persistence I would have in adulthood.

"Life is not always a bed of roses".

By five years old, I was already demonstrating a sharp mind. I was reading books from beginning to end, my eyes sweeping over pages at a speed that was shocking even for my schoolteachers. I wasn't a good writer; my handwriting was a scrawl that made me end up schooling but spelling and reading were my strong hobby.

Life of an Unknown Lady

I approached school plays in the same manner, enjoying being in the limelight and delivering dialogue confidently far in advance of my years.

I was a natural performer, and those first stage appearances planted within me a germ of ambition.

Middle school was a whirlwind of praise. I excelled in it; my teachers complimented my mind and envisioned a prosperous future for me. High school was another matter. The structure it required was in conflict with my own eccentric nature, and the entitled habits that James had fostered in me finally became apparent.

I was restless in grade nine, wondering what it was all about. We were not rich; we lived simply and did not have enough money that I would see in magazines or hear from friends. Our house had no indoor plumbing and no running water.

There was a small well in the backyard that served as our source of life, and hauling in a pail of water was a task that seemed Herculean for a girl of my height. I would go out there, pail in hand, complaining about how unfair it was.

Life of an Unknown Lady

My father was a man of unassuming strength who worked indefatigably for his family. A laborer who had hands calloused from years of hard labor, he ensured we had good food on the table and nice clothes on our backs. Never complaining, his pride in his children was evident in the way he'd beam when I showed him a good report card.

My mother was the backbone of the family. She was strict but loving and had high hopes for me because she believed in me. She envisioned a future in which I would surpass what we were living.

But I was stubborn and decided when I was fifteen that I would change the trajectory of my life by dropping out of high school. It wasn't a poor choice stemming from laziness or ineptness. I was still the girl who could read faster like speed of light and but of an erroneous notion that school wasn't for me to learn in my own way.

I had learned growing up that we didn't have enough and that because we didn't have luxuries. We must somehow be less in resources. I believed I could carve out my own destiny, make my own impression if I didn't have to sit through yet another lesson in algebra or study of history.

My mother was shocked by seeing my ability to read. My mother had given up so much in order for me to have an improved existence and couldn't understand why I would abandon it. To her, I was wasting a gift, betraying what she had perceived in me since I was a young girl.

I can recall my mother's reaction when I informed her in disappointment laced with anger. There perhaps was a slap or two given in our home, an unusual event, but what hurt most was her silence. She didn't utter a word for days and her disapproval carried a more painful load than punishment ever would.

My youth, though it had its struggles, was its own crucible that tested and tempered my character. The love of family under James's permissiveness, my father's unwavering provision, my mother's unshakable faith in me provided me with a source of strength. But it was struggles and hardships that instilled in me with resilience.

Drawing water from the well, dealing with disappointment from my parents, and struggling against my own short-sighted decisions molded me into one capable of confronting adversity squarely though not always wisely.

Life of an Unknown Lady

My first great choice in life was dropping out of high school, one that set an unseen course for me. It would not be the last. Standing on the threshold of adulthood, larger challenges lay in wait, ones that would challenge not only me but also the dynamics of our family.

It was 1962, and I was seventeen years old. My mother, younger sister, and my Aunt Clara had been a spark in all of our lives. She was the aunt who snuck her cookies into my hand when my mother was distracted, who spoke of her journeys and adventures in hushed tones with a mischievous glint in her eye.

Clara was just thirty-two when she became sick, a disease catching her off guard like a whirlwind. The doctors diagnosed it as pneumonia, but for us, it was grief that shook my entire family and laid us into the dark night. Clara's death was a shock that stunned my mother, her despair weighing heavily around her shoulders like a dark shroud.

I had never seen my mother so shattered. She had always been the rock of our family, holding us together no matter what. When Clara died, my mother was heartbroken, and for a while she lost her senses. She sat by the window gazing out into the backyard, her hands slack in her lap.

Life of an Unknown Lady

My father attempted to console my mother, but his words didn't help. James, who was on leave from service, was lost as well, his usual optimism lost in sorrow. Me? I was helpless, a child once more, not knowing what to do for her.

Those were dark times when I learned what resilience really meant. The sorrow didn't get the best of my mom. By and by, she slowly came back from it that severe loss. She'd hum while she cooked, her voice whisper-soft but unshakeable.

My mother sits through each evening with me, talking about Clara as a child, laughing and crying together. I learned from her that strength wasn't about not falling but about rising up after falling, even when loss weighed heavily.

But Clara's death was not the sole trial we endured. The early sixties saw economic hardship descend on our town. Family jobs were short, and my father saw his hours cut back in the factory. The money became even tighter, and the humble existence we were accustomed to became even more bare bones.

Life of an Unknown Lady

We consumed more soups and stews and stretched what ingredients we had to their breaking point. My mother sewed for others in order to make ends meet, her fingers deftly mending neighbors' garments. I soon joined in as well, doing odd jobs, baby-sitting, cleaning houses for pay, anything to help take some weight off from my family.

Those years were proving ground. I wasn't the pampered little princess who didn't want her vegetables anymore. Quitting school had matured me quickly, and what we were going through as a family had taught me about hard work and making sacrifices. I learned to respect my parents differently from just being careful.

I learned to see them as warriors who struggled daily in order for us to have a life. Their love, their persistence, became my strength and directed me through my own uncertain future.

I got a job as a clerk in a local general store when I was nineteen. The job was a good match for my sharp mind and brought some charm into my life. The job wasn't glamorous, but it was honest labor and for the first time in my life, I had a sense of accomplishment in helping to support my family.

Life of an Unknown Lady

The store was bustling with activity, the sound of people chattering and coins clinking. I learned to balance books, keep inventory, and get through difficult customers with a friendly smile. It was where I began getting my confidence back, where I believed, I would manage to make a place for myself in spite of previous missteps.

My mom, always vigilant, had seen the change in me. One evening while we sat on the porch shelling peas together, she grasped my hand in hers and squeezed it.

"You are finding your way, Chelock," she told me, her voice filled with warmth and pride.

"You always were stubborn, but perhaps that is not entirely a bad thing."

She had come as close as she would come to forgiving me for having quit school, and her words hung around me like an eye-opening time for me.

Life went on, each day a combination of routine and discovery. James wed a gentle woman named Lily, and the birth of Tommy, his first child, a boy, gave new life to our family. My father's body started weakening, his years of backbreaking labor finally catching up on him, but he would not give away. My mom, more resilient than ever before, was the family bond that kept us together, her strength in times of adversity a shining light.

As I entered my twenties, I was on the threshold of a new chapter. The seeds of my humble roots of my family's love, stubborn resilience of mine, lessons learned in loss and hardship that had been planted. I was no longer that teenager who had quit high school for no reason.

I was Chelock, a woman of hardships, a product of hard-won experience who was prepared for any problems that lay ahead in my life.

I had no idea that the best tests were yet ahead. The world was transforming, and in its wake, our family would have upheavals for which we would need all we had. But at that moment, standing on the porch with my mother, the future seemed like a promise rather than a threat. I was eager to confront it, having learned from what had gone before and having within me the unshakeable love of those who had nurtured me.

Chapter 2: Mother's Trials and Resurgence

Everyone has an experience in their lifetime that defines who they are. These are embedded in memory so deeply that even years after they occurred, remain as vivid as if they had just taken place.

One of my own first memories is one of my own mothers not the robust, caring woman who would come to inspire me but a weakened, frail figure who bore little resemblance to the one I would come to know. That presence in my mind would become a pillar in my appreciation for resilience, for love, and for what is understood but not articulated in what it means for a mother.

I was just two years old when I first realized that something was wrong. My mother lost a baby in a miscarriage before my birth and another one after I was born. At that age, I had no idea what her loss meant or what her sorrow was about.

All I sensed was a thread of sadness that hung over our home like thunder that smothered heavily that permeated it.

My mom, who had always been given over to laughter, a melody that played through our home was tender and weak. Her body damaged from sadness and sickness seemed to betray who she was. She would call out for me in a soft yet pleading voice, her arms open and eager for a hug. I would not go though. Not because I didn't love her, but because I was scared.

She no longer resembled my mother anymore. Her face had changed her cheeks hollow, her skin pale, her body exhausted and frail. Her eyes, which had shone brightly once with mischief and warmth, had darkened in an unhappiness that seemed to consume all light. To my child's mind, she was a different woman.

I would shake my head and back away from her, not knowing that she was suffering in ways that I couldn't perceive. I didn't know that by resisting her, fueled as it was by fear and misunderstanding, I was increasing her suffering. I couldn't know that she was reaching for me not for solace only, but to pin herself into the love we shared, to remind her that she was yet a mother while her heart was breaking.

Now that I am an adult and have had my own experiences of love and loss, I know just how much hurt she had been through not just physically, but emotionally. Losing a child is a grief no mother should ever have to endure, and my mother had lost two. The load must have been crushing her, yet she bears that dark shadow of life.

Our circumstances did not permit her the luxury of grieving out in the open. There were bills to pay, a home to manage, and a toddler in need of her care. So, she buried her profound sorrow in her bones instead of her words. She never mentioned the babies she lost, never allowed her hurt to overflow into complaints or tears in my presence. She just moved forward one stubborn step after another, her resilience, a quiet power that sustained our family.

As I matured, I became able to see more of what my mother had been through. The miscarriages had weakened her body and given her a fragility that persisted for years. There were days she moved slowly; her steps guarded as if her body were a fragile container that would break if subjected to an excessive amount of pressure. And yet she never gave up.

My mother prepared meals cleaned the house and cared for my needs with a persistence that seemed a form of defiance against her physical weakness.

There were also days when she sat for hours in stunned silence, lost in thought, her eyes driven off in some interior place far from my comprehension. I would sit in a different part of the room and watch her, trying to imagine what she was thinking about, what memories or hopes she was replaying. Even then, I sensed that her silence contained tales she would never tell.

My mother never gave up being a mother despite her struggles. She loved raising me intensely, but discipline was her bedrock. I was not an easy child. A spoiled little girl, I had a stubbornness about me, a need to push limits and test boundaries.

My mother had an unlimited capacity for patience, but when I pushed her too far, her final act of way out was always spanking. These were infrequent occurrences, but an impression they made not one of fear, but of understanding.

Even as a child, I understood she wasn't spanking me because she was angry. She was teaching me, molding me into someone who would make good choices in life, someone who would navigate life's illnesses with integrity and strength. Her discipline was an extension of her love, a means of getting me ready for a world that wouldn't always treat me kindly.

Aside from the emotional and physical strain of her losses, my mother had other difficulties that I didn't fully understand until I became older. We weren't wealthy. My father worked long hours, and my mother kept the house on a tight budget, making every dollar stretch for what we required. There were times when she didn't get new clothes, a minute's rest, or even a meal if it meant that I would have more.

Life of an Unknown Lady

She never complained, never hinted that she was giving something up. For my mother, it was just what mothers do. Her selflessness was an act of unassuming bravery that I didn't appreciate when I was a child but recognized as a demonstration of her character today.

What I marveled at most, as I looked back on those years, was that my mother never allowed her suffering to define her. The miscarriages, the sorrow, the physical war and tears were all part of her narrative but not letting anyone know about her feelings of pain. She continued by moving in life, raising me in much the same way she had been able all along.

My mother didn't get stuck on what had been or stuck in what might have been. She chose instead to live in what it was, to build a life for both of us as rich in possibility and love as her life had been beforehand. Her resilience wasn't boisterous or flamboyant; it was constant and unwavering, like a stream cutting its channel like an anchor.

As I matured into adolescence, I learned more about what my mother had been through. I became able to see the extent of her sacrifices, putting her own needs on hold in order for mine to come first. I also began feeling guilty about those early times when I had pushed her away from me, not able to approach her with friendly nature.

I wished I had been able to go back and revise those times; to run into her arms and tell her I loved her, that I saw her hurt even if I didn't know what to call it. I wished I had been able to tell her what an inspiration she was to me through her strength despite suffering such losses even though I had no words to name it.

Those wishes intensified as I became an adult and confronted my own obstacles. Life has a tendency of challenging us, of throwing walls in our way that make us have to reach inside ourselves for strength that we didn't even know we possessed. When I had my first heartbreak, it was my mother who helped see me through. I recalled how she had survived in my tragedies and not shattered, and I told myself that I would do the same as my mother did.

When I became a mother myself, those same lessons from her became even deeper. I had my own struggles, late nights spent lying awake, the crushing weight of being responsible for caring for a small life, fear of never being quite good enough and I thought of her. I thought about how she had continued through her sorrow, about how she had never let it hinder her from being the mother I needed her to be. Her strength became mine, a source I was able to draw from whenever I was depleted.

Becoming a mother also helped me see differently the sorrow my mother must have experienced after her miscarriages. I couldn't even conceive of losing a baby, the emptiness in my chest would have left.

And yet my mother had endured that loss twice and still had the strength to love me deeply, to give herself over to raising me in spite of her own hurt felt sorrows. That changed my respect for her even more. And it made me wish once more that I had been able to comfort her in those first years, to give her the love and tenderness she had so desperately required.

As time went on, I made a conscious effort to express my appreciation for my mother that I had been unable to do growing up. I told her I loved her, told her how her strength had formed me. I thanked her for her sacrifices, for the lessons she had taught me and for her love that never faltered even in her tough times. She would smile, wave off my words with a modest sweep of her hand, but in her eyes, I saw that she was moving forward in life. Those talks were my attempt to catch up on time I had lost, to pay respect to the woman who had given me everything.

My mother's tale is not an unusual one. Millions of mother's bear secrets that they never share while suffering in silence and hardship for the benefit of their children. Yet my mother's story is inextricably woven into my being. Her hardship sowed seeds of fortitude within me that sprouted and flourished as I walked my own way in life.

With every challenge that confronts me, I reflect on her uncomplaining strength, her unfailing love, her refusal to be defeated by hurt. I reflect on the woman who stretched out her hand for me even while she was shattering, who loved me even when I was terrified of loving her in return.

Now, raising my own children, I try my best to live out what my own mother taught me. I want them to see in me that same strength, that same love, that same resolve to keep moving no matter what life sends my direction. I want them to see that hurt is a part of life, but it doesn't have to shape us. We can bear it, learn from it, and come out stronger as a result of it. And I want them to see that love is the anchor of it all, fierce love, unconditional love and abiding love.

Life of an Unknown Lady

At times, I catch myself gazing at my children and wondering what memories they will take away from growing up. Will they retain awareness of the late nights? I spent time worrying about being the best mother she deserves. Will they bear in mind those times when I stumbled, when my own problems made me short of perfect? Will they instead live in remembrance of the love, laughter, and times when we worked through difficulties as a team and emerged stronger?

I hope it is these things. I hope they see in me what I saw in my own mother a woman who, flaws and hardships notwithstanding, never gave up trying and never gave up loving.

My mother had a fair share of sorrow in life, but hers was also a life of victory. She had survived her losses, her suffering, and her hardships and created a life rich in love and purpose. She taught me that strength is not about the absence of weakness but about having the courage to persevere in spite of it.

My mother proved to me that love can survive even the deepest wounds, that it heals and reconstructs what sorrow has destroyed. And she blessed me with resilience; a gift that I live with daily.

Life of an Unknown Lady

As I reflect on those early recollections of the dying woman who grasped for me, of that sorrow that clung about our home no longer do I experience the guilt and regret once associated with them. Rather, I am filled with gratitude. Gratitude for a mother who loved me in spite of her suffering, who taught through her example, who molded me into who I am today.

Her travail was not for naughty. It was in the crucible in which my own strength was tempered, in which I have built my life.

At its core, my mother's story is one of resilience, of love, of unspoken bravery. A story that lives within me, not simply in recollections, but in daily living. A story that I hope I can share with my own children, that they might know what it means to persevere, what it means to love and what it means to keep moving forward despite everything.

A story that I'll tell over and over again, in order to keep alive, the one who gave me life and taught me that no matter what darkness we are living through, we can get through it.

Chapter 3: Dreams Deferred

Dreams are strange things. They begin as small seeds in the depths of one's heart, those seeds being hard to detect in the beginning. At times, they are nurtured and grow large, flowering into visions so richly detailed that they occupy one's ever thought. Some remain idle and wait for a spark that never appears.

Sometimes dreams remain just dreams. Hawaii was one of those for me. A destination I had always dreamed of visiting, far away and enchanting and out of reach. I had clung to that dream through years when it seemed out of reach. And today I am content just to let it go.

I was in my early years in school when I first envisioned Hawaii between first and sixth grade, about eleven years old. Memories of those years are fuzzy, as if through a fogged windowpane, but some stick out in my mind clearly and sharply. Our school would produce plays, often Wednesday nights, and those nights were my favorites.

"Ah! what an opportunity it was to experience an entirely different world for a while."

Everything about the stage, the costumes, and music was alive, full of potential.

One time we learned a Hawaiian dance for one of those productions. I don't know where it had come from, perhaps a teacher had seen it somewhere or had been told about it by a friend.

Whatever it was, we learned it in school and moved in time, our hips swaying and arms waving in soft flowing motions. When performance time rolled around, I recall stepping out onto that stage, warm lights in my face, and music enveloping me in a soft caress. Oh, it was stunning the beauty of the tune, the movement of ourselves.

I was somewhere else during those minutes, for a moment I forgot I was just some children from a small school. I was elsewhere, far away and magical. I was in Hawaii, a place I had never been to but somehow understood in my soul.

That evening something changed in me. Hawaii was no longer simply a location on a map. It was a dream, an aspiration that had settled in my chest. I did not know anything really except that it was distant, stunning, and that people danced there like we had danced that evening.

I wished to go and see it for myself, to feel the sand, hear the music, and breathe in the air. I didn't have a grand aspiration. I didn't want to live there or build a life. I simply wanted to go there for a visit, meet its people, see its dances and hear its music.

Life has a tendency to get in the way of dreams, though. As I got older, things got busier. School loaded up on homework, then part-time jobs, family obligations, and all the little things that pack a life. The dream of Hawaii didn't disappear entirely, per se, but it pushed its way into the back of my mind, where it sat on a shelf collecting dust. I didn't think about it nearly as often anymore, and when I did it seemed more like a memory rather than an option. Eventually I gave up.

"Oh well, that isn't going to occur. So, what's the use in thinking about it?"

Hawaii wasn't a profound symbolic place for me. It didn't represent freedom or adventure or a fresh start. It was simply about seeing something beautiful, something different. I loved having danced it, and I thought it would be impressive to see it in the land in which it was meant to exist. A small dream, yes, but one that lingered in a secluded part of my heart.

Even today, if I sit back and think about it, I can still feel the enchantment of that evening on stage. I can hear the music, feel the beat of the dance, see the glow of lights. I was in Hawaii for an instant, bathed in beauty. And that instant was sufficient to sustain the dream for years even if it never became reality.

Life of an Unknown Lady

Sometimes dreams remain just dreams. I am a dreamer. I have had plenty of dreams in my lifetime, some large in scope, some small, some that worked out and some that didn't. Hawaii is one that got away from me, and I've reconciled myself to that.

I was eleven when it first planted its seeds in my mind, and decades have come and gone since then. I know it isn't going to happen. I'm an older person now and have had different routes in life. I don't mind. I've released it, and there's a sort of liberty in that.

Occasionally, though, I do wonder about it. What would it have been like to have stood on a Hawaiian shore, to have seen the waves come in, to have witnessed dances under starlight? Would it have been as enchanting as I had dreamed it would be, or would it have been different and imperfect but real? I'll never know and that is alright.

Dreams don't have to come true for them to mean something. Sometimes they are in place simply to inspire hope in you, to make you feel alive and remind you that the world is full of amazing potential.

I've had other dreams as well through the years. Dreams of family and love and watching my children grow. Some of those dreams were answered in ways I never even imagined. Some shattered into a thousand pieces and left scars that healed slowly.

None of those dreams I regret. Every single one of them taught a lesson. Whether they were answered or not, they taught me something. To keep going, no matter what. To hope. To dream.

My Hawaii dream was significant because it was one of my first. It was conceived in an instant of pure excitement, in a place where I had a feeling of being able to do anything, going anywhere. Even once I released it, it stayed in my mind, a memory of little girl wonders and possibility. The dream provided me with something to hold on to, even if I was never able to get to those islands.

In retrospect, I see how significant dreams are even when they do not become reality. The dreams are not about the destination but about the journey. The dreams are about the thrill, about the hope, about an improved feeling that comes from closing one's eyes and envisioning something more and something different. Even if a dream never comes to pass, it is significant. It influences one; it propels one forward; it moves one in one direction or another.

Hawaii taught me two important lessons that remain with me today. The first is that it is okay to dream even if those dreams do not ultimately work out. The second is that it is okay to hold onto something even when you realize it may never occur. Dreams are not always about accomplishing goals, but about hope. Dreams are about keeping in mind that things are possible even if circumstances go against them.

I often think about that little girl growing up, who danced that Hawaiian dance and imagined far-off islands. I think about how her heart expanded with possibility, about how she imagined she might go anywhere, see anything. That little girl is still inside of me today. She reminds me to keep on dreaming, keep on hoping, keep searching for beauty in the world.

Perhaps another person has had my dream. Perhaps they'll stand on a Hawaiian beach and see the dancers, hear the music, feel the warm air on their skin. Perhaps they'll remember a little girl who dreamed about that once long ago, and perhaps that's all that matters. Dreams tend to bring people together, to inspire hope in one another's hearts, to make the world a smaller place, a brighter place.

Dreams are strange things. They begin small, but they can become something that transforms you. They can linger after you release them. And sometimes they are not about getting someplace at all, but about the way they make you feel, about reminding you that everything is possible. Hawaii was one of those dreams for me, and I am thankful for it. It gave me hope, gave me joy, and reminded me that it is never wasted time to dream.

Now that I think about that dream, I know it wasn't really about Hawaii. It was about experiencing something outside of my mundane reality, something alive and vibrant. That Hawaiian dance provided my first glimpse of that something different from my usual surroundings yet appealing.

The window that allowed me a glimpse of a completely different civilization from what I was familiar with yet somehow welcoming.

I carried that curiosity in the years that elapsed. Even when visions of Hawaii receded, the need to see new places, meet new people, and experience new things became intense. I didn't get to Hawaii, but I discovered alternative means of satisfying that appetite for discovery. I traveled whenever I was able to sometimes to places nearby, other times farther off. Every trip, no matter its size, was a small fulfillment of that initial dream.

There was once when I traveled to a seaside town a short ride from home where the air had a salty scent and waves lapped against rocky outcrops. Not Hawaii, it erupted on a sandy beach instead, but it longed for another realm. I stood, gazing at water, and remembered that evening on stage, how music had transported me someplace far away. That moment by the sea recalled a spark of that same sensation, possibility, loveliness.

Another evening, I attended a cultural celebration in a neighboring city. The dancers were from all corners of the globe and danced under shining lights, moving in a story I couldn't grasp completely but sensed in my very bones.

A group danced a traditional Polynesian dance, and for an instant, I was eleven once more, dancing to a Hawaiian tune. I closed my eyes and let music transport me back onto that school stage and back into that dream that once burned within me.

Life of an Unknown Lady

Those fleeting seconds, tiny as they were, reminded me that dreams don't need to be grand in order to make a difference. They don't need to transport you around the globe in order to transform. Sometimes they are in mundane things like a song, a dusk, a recollection that catches you by surprise. They are in the way in which you are able to see the earth, open-eyed for its loveliness even when you are not moving.

I have had other dreams throughout the years, some larger than Hawaii and some smaller. There was a dream of having a family, of having a home with love and laughter in it. That one became reality in ways I didn't anticipate messy, imperfect, but real.

There was a dream of having a career that meant something, a career that allowed me to make a difference in some small way. That one was slower in arriving, with lots of detours in between, but I made it through eventually.

And then those dreams that had not panned out. The ones that fell through my fingers, Hawaii being one of them. The dream of an intact, unbroken family. The dream of never having lost one whom I loved. These dreams broke if they did not come through, but they had taught me about resilience. They had taught about what is left after shattered dreams lessons, strength, and enhanced awareness of what it is to be human.

Hawaii, however, is still a child's dream. Never about proving anything or accomplishing something. Never about chasing beauty for its own ends. That was what made it so pure, untainted by the influences of the outside world. It was a child's dream, created in an instance of happiness and it retained its element of happiness even as it dissolved.

Occasionally I think about returning to that eleven-year-old girl and being able to tell her that she wouldn't make it to Hawaii. Would she be disappointed? Would she feel as though she'd lost? I don't believe so. I believe that she'd realize, in her own mind, that the dream had never been about to arrive. It had been about the manner in which it made her feel alive, full of hope, part of something larger than herself.

That is what dreams do. Dreaming ignites a spark within you, and even if the spark may not turn into a flame, it does leave a warmth that lingers within you. Dreaming provides you with something to clutch onto when everything else seems heavy.

Life of an Unknown Lady

I have learned to appreciate that warmth, and I actively go in pursuit of it in little things each day. It is in the sun shining through the trees in my backyard and casting its patterns on the lawn. It is in my children laughing even in those days when parenting was an uphill battle. It is in music I play when I must get away, music that causes my heart to swing as it once did on stage years ago.

Hawaii might have remained out of sight, but it did something just as precious for me. It educated me on how to dream fearlessly, hope unwaveringly, pursue beauty even when one does not know where one is going. It taught me that dreams, even those that don't work out, are not wasted. They mold you; they lead you; they remind you who you are.

And who knows? Perhaps one day, another person will live that dream for me. Perhaps they would stand on a Hawaiian shore, observing dancers, listening to the beat of the islands. Perhaps they would inherit a fragment of my dream and not even realize it.

And perhaps that is the true magic of dreams that don't belong just to you. They fan out, touching people that you have never met, igniting hope in hearts that you have never mentioned.

Life of an Unknown Lady

So, I persist in dreaming. I dream about new lands, new adventures, new epiphanies. I dream of a life where my children can pursue their own dreams, having no fear of what may or may not happen. I dream of mornings spent experiencing little pleasures, and peaceful nights. And I cling to those dreams, not because they are all going to happen, but because they make living worth the while.

Hawaii was my original dream and in some sense it still lingers. It's in how I navigate through life, always searching for beauty, always available for possibility. It's in the manner in which I encourage my children to dream, to hope, to believe in something more. And it's in those quiet times when I shut my eyes and can hear the melody of that far-distant dance and am transported back to a place I've never been, but one I'll always adore.

Dreams are peculiar things. They begin small, but they have a way of growing into something that transforms you completely. They linger in your heart, even if and when you release them. And sometimes they have nothing to do with getting to where they lead, but they are about the way they make you feel, about reminding you that life holds endless possibilities, waiting to be dreamed.

Chapter 4: Building Family of Her Own

I had learned a long time ago that life doesn't always abide by the script that you write for it. When I was 16 and I became pregnant, it was an unexpected twist that turned my life around. To say that it wasn't part of my plan is an understatement. I was a teenager, still trying to figure out who I was, let alone becoming a mother.

But life doesn't wait for you to get ready for it, and I had to confront this reality head on. Far from allowing it to break me, I decided to go forward one step at a time.

At 17, I gave birth to my second child, and that was when the struggles really kicked in. Young and unsure and in my head, I didn't have a clear vision for the future, but I did know one thing: I cared for my children, and I would do whatever it took in order for them to have a good life.

Becoming a 16-year-old mother was being plunged into the deep end of a pool with no swimming lessons. I was still a teenager myself, trying to get through high school, make friends, and live out those teenage fantasies of adventure and independence. And then I had a baby who needed to be cared for by a tiny human who relied on my every need. The sleepless nights, diaper changes for what seemed like an endless time, and the constant fear that I was doing everything wrong. There have been times when I have been completely alone thinking about how I would get through.

With my second child just a year after that, the responsibilities doubled. One under two and one under one and I'm just 18 years old. The sheer managerial task of balancing doctor's visits and feedings and naptimes was intimidating on its own.

I relied desperately on my family for help, particularly my mom, who became my pillar. She didn't sugarcoat reality about the difficulties but quietly encouraged her and gave practical assistance whenever needed. She helped remind me that I wasn't completely alone even when it seemed that way.

In spite of the turmoil, there were times of raw joy that kept me from falling apart. My daughter's first smile, my son's little hand curled around my own finger, there were flashes of light in the darkness. These reminded me that I was doing what I was doing for a reason, even on the toughest days. I wasn't just getting through it all; I was creating a family, albeit one that was unplanned.

Marriage was not in my immediate plan either. I was 17 and in New York trying to figure out what I was doing next, and my children's father was in West Columbia. We were both young and inexperienced and had a long-distance relationship with two children involved. We didn't know all of the answers by far. We were determined to make it happen for the benefit of our children though.

One day, he picked up the phone and offered a practical proposal, not a fairy-tale one: *"Come home and we can get married."* It wasn't fairy tale, but it was right. I moved back to West Columbia, and we were wed.

Our wedding was modest, no frills, but it changed everything. We were no longer two children just playing at the house; we were a family committed to giving security to our children.

Marriage also had its own set of obstacles. We were both so inexperienced and still figuring out who we were as people, let alone as couples. There were fights and miscommunications and times when I questioned if we had made the right decision. We had one goal in common, though: providing a stable, loving home for our children. That kept us in perspective even when times were difficult.

Raising two children as a young mother was a delicate balance that required constant tuning in. My husband was a stickler for discipline and propriety. He wanted his children to address him as "yes ma'am" and "no sir," to always use good manners and show respect.

Life of an Unknown Lady

His severity stemmed from a place of love where he wanted his children to have strong values and a sense of accountability. I often wanted to temper his style, though, making room for his children to know it was okay to make a mistake.

I wanted them to know they could bring me anything, no matter what. I'd sit with them in the evening, hearing about what they had been through, about what they feared and what they dreamed of.

Those times were special, reminders that love was what held together our family even when we didn't see eye-to-eye on the details. My husband and I learned about balancing each other out he gave structure, and I provided warmth. It didn't come easily all the time, but we adapted.

As they got older, things changed. The children began developing personalities of their own, their own aspirations, and, inevitably, their own problems. I did my best to be supportive while allowing them room for individual growth. Letting go was more difficult than I had anticipated. Seeing them make their own decisions, some of which I knew would hurt, which was one of the most difficult aspects of being a parent. I had to have faith that what we had taught them would see them through.

Despite all the struggles, the happy times were worth it. Every milestone was a victory step first words, first days of school. I recall my daughter's graduation from kindergarten, her little cap and gown making her appear so mature yet remain so little.

I can still see my son's first soccer game in my head, his goal and his proud glow. These were some of those times that reminded me I continued for a reason, no matter what difficulties the road might have had.

As my children matured into adulthood, I saw them chart their own course. My daughter married, and for a time it appeared she had discovered her happily-ever-after. I was proud of her for being one who believed in love and who had been brave enough to go for it.

When her marriage broke apart in divorce, though, my heart hurt for her. I wanted to protect her from the hurt, but I didn't know how. All I could do was be available, listening and providing her with a shoulder on which to cry.

Life of an Unknown Lady

My son had a similar experience. His wedding had been packed with so much hope at first but ultimately resulted in a divorce as well. I struggled watching both my children experience that kind of heartache after I had worked so diligently to build a stable home for them. I wondered if I had been able to do anything different to prepare them.

Deep inside myself, though, I knew I had given them everything I could. Life is one of those things that knows its own lessons and sometimes those lessons include hurt.

Reflecting back, I am surprised at just how far I have traveled. I was a nervous teenage girl at 16 years old, fearing what lay ahead. I confronted it, nonetheless, creating a life for my children and for myself. It was not effortless, though -- it involved late nights, financial hardships, and times of self-doubt. There were also days of laughter, family rituals, and unbreakable love.

If I had my time over, I don't know if I would have become a mother at 16. Not that I don't adore them, I do more than anything but because it was just so difficult. As a 16-year-old mother, I had to mature quicker than I was capable of, accepting responsibilities that were more than a little daunting at times. Yet I wouldn't part with my children for anything.

My husband was my best friend throughout it all, my biggest love. We created a life that wasn't perfect but was our own. We struggled to give our children a good life, to teach them right from wrong, to teach them what it means to stick it out. We didn't always succeed, but we did the best we could with what we had. And in the end, that is all anyone can do.

Being that age meant having to grow up as an adult while caring for two little ones who were counting on me. There were times when it seemed too much when exhaustion, worry, and uncertainty pushed us against being able to manage.

I got through it one day at a time though, drawing on my husband in times of need for what strength I needed and returning the support for him as well. We worked as a unit through the highs and lows.

The issues changed as time passed. It was about survival in the beginning, making certain that the children were fed, dressed, and protected. As they matured, it was about directing them, assisting in navigating school, friends, and even dreams. And as adults, it was about relinquishing, knowing that they would make it through even if I couldn't shield them from all of it.

One of the most challenging lessons was accepting that I couldn't protect them from suffering in life. When my daughter's marriage broke up, I wanted to mend it for her, erase her hurt. When my son had his own issues, I wished I could intervene and make everything fine. Part of being a parent means knowing when to step aside, when to let your children fight their own fights. Something I am still learning.

Through everything, family has been my grounding. The love we have, the memories we've made are what matter most. Family life is messy and imperfect and occasionally heart-wrenching, but it is beautiful.

It is late nights rocking an ailing child to bed, early mornings cheering in the stands at a soccer game, tears of laughter around the table during meals. It is sacrifices made in an instant, struggles that make the victories that are much sweeter.

Life of an Unknown Lady

Family is what carries you through. Family is what gives you the strength to go on when you want to quit, the courage to leap forward into unknowns, and the joy that makes living worthwhile. My children and my husband provided me with purpose, a reason for continuing even when the odds seemed against me. They are everything, my heart and my legacy.

Now that I've looked back on my journey, I realize that I see lessons I have learned throughout. I have learned that things do not always go as planned but that that doesn't mean they can't be beautiful. I have learned that love is the building block of it all love for your children, for your spouse, for yourself. I have learned that errors are a part of growing and that resilience is formed through hardship.

I have learned as well about forgiveness not only for others but for oneself. There have been times when I thought I'd been a failure as a mother when I questioned if I'd been able to do more. I have since learned that being a parent is not about being perfect but about loving and being supportive of one's children. I did that and I am proud of it.

To anyone who is also having an unexpected adventure of some sort --whether it's an unplanned pregnancy or some other surprise challenge --I want to say this: You are stronger than you think. Get through one day at a time, lean on those who care about you deeply, and don't hesitate to ask for help if you need it. Life might not go as planned, but it can still be rich and full of love and purpose.

My children are grown up now and have lives of their own, experiencing joys and struggles. I'm still around for them, just as I have been all along, but I've learned to let them take flight. They are not perfect, and neither am I, but we're family, held together by love and shared experiences.

My husband and I have aged together, our union tested by time but made stronger through mutual commitment. We've laughed and cried and constructed a life that isn't what I envisioned for myself 16 years ago but is my life nonetheless and one I wouldn't trade.

It is all worth it for those times of connection, those times of laughter, and those times of proud silence while observing your children grow. It is worth it for that love that sustains it all, that love that makes everything else lose its importance.

At the end of it all, my children are my greatest achievement, and my husband is my greatest love. Together we have created a life that is imperfect but beautiful, challenging but fulfilling. It is ours, and that is all that really counts.

Chapter 5: Heartbreak and Healing

The heart is a delicate vessel that can hold cruelty and love in equal measures. For my youngest son, who died at forty-eight years old, his passing severely affects my soul with anguish and more painful than anything else. It was heartbreak that rewrote my character, tested my patience, and revealed truths about living, dying, and the quiet resilience necessary to move forward. This is the story of that journey and the moment when everything has changed in my life.

Life of an Unknown Lady

I had to confronted that the grief followed and discovered is meant to be live through an unimaginable loss. I had three children; Cindy Linton, Clara Mitchell and Carl Mitchell who sleep in Jesus. And I believe that on the rebirth of life in Jesus as mentioned in Holy Scriptures.

It was a Saturday evening, starting like any other day, yet ending with a burden that would stay with me forever. My son had battled seizures for years.

It was an illness that kept me in constant tension, always watching and bothering me from inside. My son lived alone, and although he had doctor's care at times when no one else could be there and that's why my fear persisted.

On that evening, I called my son, as I often did, just to talk and hear his voice. The phone rang and rang, but he did not answer. A mother's intuition that something was terribly wrong.

I ran to his home, my heart racing with each mile. When I opened the door and went to his bedroom, the world stopped and changed me forever. There was my son lying dead. He had been gone for more than a day, his body also started decomposing. Shock froze me in place where I was standing. I was unable to grasp reality. The police arrived after I called them and took him away for an autopsy.

Life of an Unknown Lady

Arrangements for the funeral were made, but all my mind could focus on was that my son, my fourth son, was no longer in this world.

I chose to keep the funeral closed to protect his memory and spare others the pain of seeing him in that condition. Some did not understand; they thought it was wrong, especially since he was well-known and loved in our community.

My son's classmates, spoken about their grief, wanted to say their goodbyes. But I could not bear the thought of him being remembered that way. I wanted them to hold onto the vibrant, kind man he had been, with the memories he left behind. It was one of the hardest choices I ever made, but it was mine to make as his mother.

His death sent ripples through our family, not as I expected. We had always been close, bound by love and shared struggles, but grief revealed cracks in our family foundation. My other children grieved in their own ways, but we did not rally together as I had hoped.

There were no long speeches, no tears shed collectively to bind us closer. Instead, an unspoken distance appeared, as though each of us was grappling with the loss in our own isolated world.

His own family, two daughters and a toddler son were deeply affected. His daughters, grown women forging their own paths, bore their grief with stoic acceptance. His youngest child, barely old enough to know his father, attended the funeral with his mother.

I saw confusion in their eyes, a struggle to understand a loss that they could not fully grasp. I wanted to hold them, to tell them about their father. They would never know, but words tumbled me. Our family felt shattered not by anger or blame, but by the weight of the space he left behind.

To my surprise, support came from my son's classmates. They stood beside me in a way that caught me off guard, paying for and planning his funeral when there was no insurance to cover the cost. Their graciousness moved me to people who had not seen him in decades came together to remember his laughter, kindness, and appearance.

They stood with me when I needed them most, their support like a rope keeping me from drowning. In an odd way, their affection for my son showed me that family is not always blood related; it is the people who stand up with you when your world crumbles.

Grief is a strange beast; it does not always manifest as expected. I did not weep endlessly or hide away. I did not talk about it much, either. Instead, I plodded through the tasks: arranging the funeral ceremony, thanking those who helped and putting things in order. It was as though my body knew it had to keep moving, even when my heart wanted to stop.

Emotionally, I felt hollow, as if part of me had been carved out. Mentally, I paced through "what-ifs": What if I had called sooner? What if the doctors had done more? Physically, I was drained, carrying an exhaustion that went beyond sleepless nights.

But I did not linger in those places too long. I missed my son terribly, his voice, his presence, the way he was always there for me, more than my other sons. But I could not let myself be anguished. I had other children, grandchildren, a life that still needed me. I had no rituals or coping strategies, not the ones people might expect.

No morning prayers, no journaling, no walks in the woods for relief. I just kept moving and moving at that time. The funeral was my sole focus, a way to honor him and provide closure for those who loved him. After that, it was my routine to clean my house, checking in with family and getting things done. It was not healing yet; it was surviving on my own.

Life of an Unknown Lady

At times, stories from his classmates offered fleeting comfort, their memories painting a picture of a well-lived life. Those exchanges, though rare, were small anchors, keeping me afloat when grief threatened to pull me under. I also found solace in silence. I spoke little of my pain, not because I did not feel it, but because words failed me communicate even with myself.

I kept my son in my heart, sustained by the love we shared. It was not a deliberate plan, but it was mine a quiet personal way of holding him close while still living each day with his memories.

Over the months, I began seeking meaning, though unconsciously. I did not find solace in religion or any other activity, as others might. Nature did not call me, nor did music or creativity. Yet, there were small, fleeting moments that offered a glimpse of something more: a conversation with my son's classmate sharing a memory I had not known, a quiet moment alone when I could almost feel him nearby. These were not earth-shattering, but they sustained me.

The hardest part was the misunderstanding from those who judged my decision to keep the casket closed, believing I was denying them closure. Their words stung, not because they were cruel, but because they did not see the love behind my choice.

What sustained me were the acts of kindness: classmates who contributed to the funeral, friends who called just to check in, strangers who offered respect after the service. Those actions reminded me I was not alone, even when it felt that way.

Losing my son taught me about life's fragility. It shows me quickly that memories cannot vanish, and how little control we have on ourselves. It showed me that death does not end love it lingers in memories, stories, and the people who carry a piece of that person with them.

It taught me about resilience not the loud triumphant kind, but the persistent kind that gets you out of bed each morning. I learned that moving on does not mean forgetting. It means carrying the loss with you, letting it shape you without breaking you.

My son's passing also revealed the power of community. His peers, who stepped up when no one else did, showed me that people can surprise you with generosity. The people can appear from unexpected places. It made me more present with those around me, more grateful for the time we share with each other.

Life of an Unknown Lady

I began to cherish the trivial things: moments of laughter, everyday interactions and the simple act of living.

My grief evolved over time. It did not disappear, but it softened, becoming part of who I am, not all of who I am. There were no epiphanies, no single moment when the pain lifted from my heart.

Healing came in small realizations, quiet moments of acceptance. I watched my son's daughters build their lives; his older daughter married and had a son, a little boy who carries a spark of his grandfather's spirit.

Seeing that my son's child laugh marked a turning point not to instant heal me, but a reminder that life persists even in moments of grief.

I also learned to forgive myself for what I could not control. I had always been hard on myself, questioning if I could have done more as a mother. But son's death showed me that some things are beyond our control. I loved him with all my being, been there to the best of my ability, and that was not even enough for me. Freed from guilt, I could remember him with love but not regret.

My son's death transformed me in ways that are still unfolding. It deepened my sense of life's fragility and the power of love. It showed me that moving forward is not betrayal, but a way to honor the departed by living in true manners. It revealed the quiet resilience within each of us, even in the darkest times, which carries us forward and healed step by step.

Chapter 6: Journey of Perseverance

The years following my son's death were a crucible, forging an endurance I did not know I had. Life became a series of small battles with grief, loneliness, and the constant charge of survival, each needing a strength I had to summon daily.

This chapter explores the perseverance of my daily life during those challenging times, the quiet labor that kept me going, the sacrifices that shaped my growth, and the moments of forgoes that tested but defined my story of determination.

Through prayer, self-sufficiency, and the support of a small loyal community helped me in every way I wanted. I learned what it means to endure.

An ordinary day was an exercise in simplicity and survival, marked by the weight of loss and the need to carry on. I woke up early, not by choice but because sleep was elusive.

In the darkness before dawn, the stillness of my one-bedroom apartment was both comfort and a reminder of my solitude. My breakfast was simple toast, coffee, and an egg eaten standing by the window and watching the world awaken.

Those moments were for prayer, an act that anchored me. I prayed for strength to face the day and for peace to soothe the grief in my heart.

With my children growing up and living their own lives, my days no longer revolved around family routines. I did not work; my years as a stay-at-home mother had seen to that, and in my later years, I relied on modest Social Security, occasional family contributions, or the kindness of neighbors.

Life of an Unknown Lady

I was living a life only for survival: cleaning my apartment, stretching every dollar, and managing the necessities of home.

I swept floors, washed dishes, and did whatever was affordable like cooking rice, beans, or, if I could splurge, a piece of meat. These mundane tasks were my way of holding everything together.

The afternoons were the hardest when the silence in my apartment felt oppressive. Memories of my son surfaced his laughter; his presence and I struggled to keep them from overwhelming me. To stay busy, I walked to the corner store for a loaf of bread or a can of soup or sat on the porch and watched pedestrians.

Evenings were for reflection, prayer, an occasional call to one of my two close friends, or an hour listening to gospel music on the radio. I was in bed before nine, praying for sleep, though my mind often wandered to anxieties about the future or regrets about the past. It was a quiet existence, stripped of essentials, but it was mine, and I faced it one day at a time.

Though I did not work outside the home, my work was no less vital. In my earlier years, I had poured everything into my children, ensuring they had food, clothes, and a roof over their heads, even when resources were scarce.

Now, alone, my work was sustaining myself, which was its own challenge. There was no paycheck, no office, but the effort of staying afloat required relentless budgeting, mending clothes instead of replacing them, and negotiating with landlords when budget was tight.

When my children were young, I had taken on odd jobs sewing, babysitting, selling cookies to keep us going. Those small efforts had been enough then, and now that same resourcefulness sustained me.

I scoured circulars for deals, haggled with shopkeepers, and stretched meals to last days. When a neighbor offered a plate of food or a church member slipped a dollar into my hand, I accepted, though it stung my pride. This was not the life I had planned, but it was my life, and I fought to make it work for my betterment.

Emotionally, I stayed connected to my family, even from a distance. I wrote letters, called when I had free time, and prayed for their well-being. Being there for them, even in small ways, was work that needed patience and love, especially as their lives pulled them further away.

Life of an Unknown Lady

My role as a mother never ended, though it looked different now.

The sacrifices during this time were not for the family I had raised, but for my own survival and dignity. One of the greatest achievements was my independence from my own self. A car accident in my later years ended my ability to drive, a loss that held with me deeply.

I had always been self-reliant, the type to do everything by myself. Losing the ability to drive to the store, visit a friend, or go somewhere for an hour wanted to lose part of myself. Relying on others for rides, each requested a small sacrifice of the independence I had held so dear for those help me.

Another sacrifice was inner comfort. Moving from apartment to apartment with little to my name meant letting go of the dream of a stable home. Each move was a fresh start but also a reminder of how little I owned. I packed my few belongings, carrying a Bible, some clothes, a photo of my son and started over again, and abandoning hopes of stability.

I gave up the small luxury's others took for granted: new clothes, dining out and trips to see family. Every penny went toward survival.

Life of an Unknown Lady

The greatest sacrifice was my dreams. As a young girl, I had dreamed of simple things: visiting Hawaii, exploring unfamiliar places, owning a small home filled with family. Those dreams faded as life demanded my focus on the present issues.

I let go of travel, adventure, anything beyond the daily grind. It was not a dramatic loss, but a quiet one, a gradual erosion of the hopes I had once cherished.

These hardships, though painful, were a crucible for growth. I discovered that I had to be stronger than I ever knew. Life had taken my son, my independence, my dreams, yet I was still standing. That realization reshaped my sense of self. I was not just a widow or a mother; I was a woman who could endure, who could face the worst and keep going. This strength was not loud or boastful; it lived quietly in the daily choice to rise and face the world.

I also grew more patient, both with myself and with life's uncertainties. On days when isolation or grief felt heavily on me, I felt I had failed on that day. But I learned to forgive myself, to see those moments as part of being human. I came to value small victories: a day without tears, a kind word from a neighbor, and an answered prayer.

Life of an Unknown Lady

My faith deepened, not in a flashy way. Prayer became more than ritual; it was a conversation, a way to hand over burdens I could not carry alone. It taught me humility, the ability to admit I did not have all the answers. Through these trials, I became someone who could bend without breaking and who could find light in the darkness.

Failure is a harsh word, but there were moments when I felt it keenly. One came after my accident when I lost my ability to drive. It was not just the loss of mobility; it was the loss of control of independence. I had fought so hard to support myself. I remember sitting in my living room, staring at the walls, feeling I had hit rock bottom.

The world shrank to the size of my apartment, and I wondered if life had anything left for me. I felt I had futile myself and the part of me that had always found a way to persevere.

Another failure was the distance that grew between me and my children. They were adults, living their own lives, but I had always believed we would stay close, bound by the love we shared. Instead, their visits became rare, their calls became infrequent. I blamed myself, wondering if I had been unsuccessful as a mother. This estrangement felt like a personal failing, a split in the family.

But these setbacks were also turning points in my life. After the car accident, I had to redefine myself. I leaned on prayer, asking for strength to accept help and adapt to a new way of living. I started small walking to the store instead of driving, building relationships with neighbors who became my support network.

It was not the life I had envisioned, but it was a life of pain and determination. With my children, I learned to let go, to love them from afar and trust that the bonds we had built would endure, even in a different form.

I did not have a wide circle, but the support I did have was my lifeline. My church community was my enduring strength. They prayed, but they also showed up with tangible help: driving me to appointments, sharing meals, or sitting with me when loneliness struck in my home.

Their presence reminded me I was not alone. I also had two close friends, women I could call when the world felt too heavy. They did not try to fix everything; they listened, laughed with me, and reminded me of who I was.

These relationships, though few, fueled my perseverance. They taught me that asking for help is not a weakness, but strength. They showed me the power of community, of people who care enough to stand by you in the time of difficulties. Without them, I am not sure I would have made it through this day.

The challenges of those years refined my values and reshaped my identity. I came to value resilience above all the ability to weather both good times and bad, to keep going no matter what. I learned that life is made of moments, a choice to choose strength over defeat. My faith became a cornerstone, not just a belief but a practical tool for survival. I value honesty to admit when I am struggling, to accept help, to keep moving forward even when I felt spontaneous.

My identity shifted from what I had done with my mother, wife or to others. I became a woman of quiet strength and a survivor. I took pride in insignificant things: getting through a tough day, helping a struggling neighbor. These challenges taught me that identity is not about what you have or lose, but how you navigate it.

Looking back, I am proud of my perseverance. Life through so much grief, loneliness, loss of independence, yet I did not break. I prayed through every trial, every moment of doubt and every fear. That moment of faith and relentless resolve to keep going, is what I hold onto. I am proud of the woman I became, someone who could face the worst and still find reason to rise each morning with new hopes to come on my way.

I am also proud of the small victories: days without tears, laughter with a friend, helping someone else when I needed to help myself. To others, they might seem trivial, but to me, they were proof of living with courage. I had my strength, my faith, and trust in myself to keep moving in hardships of life.

Chapter 7: Generational reflections

As time passed, becoming a grandmother and great-grandmother marked a new chapter in my life. One of unexpected joy and profound responsibility. My grandchildren and great-grandchildren brightened my days, even as they challenged me to bridge generational gaps. This chapter explores the boundless joy they brought, the wisdom and values I tried to impart, and my reflections on the enduring importance of family bonds and the legacy that I wanted to leave. Family became the thread that stitches our lives together, passing love and lessons across generations.

The first time I held my granddaughter, a wave of joy sluiced over me, unlike anything I had ever felt. She was born when my daughter still lived with me, and the moment I saw her tiny face, she became a gift I had not known I needed. I gave her a nickname that stuck, and her presence brought new energy to our home.

Everyone who met her lit up, drawn to her curious gaze and quick smile. Like her grandmother, I felt pride with tender joy that anchored me against life's hardships.

Becoming a great-grandmother years later was equally profound, but with an unfamiliar perspective. My own grandparents had all passed before I was born, so I felt especially grateful to be there for my great-grandchildren. Many of them had no other grandparents or great-grandparents, making my role even more precious.

Holding each new baby, holding them gently, or watching them take their first steps filled me with quiet joy that softened the edges of grief and loneliness. These moments were brief, as their parents often moved away when the children were young, but they were priceless. Each child reminded me that life continues, that there can be growth even amidst loss.

What made these relationships special was how they connected me to the future. With each grandchild and great-grandchild, I saw my family's story extend a continuing tale of hardship, resilience, and love. I talked with them, sang to them, or simply held them, cherishing the chance to be part of their early years. Even as they grew and our time together became less frequent, those early memories remained treasures that comforted me in quieter moments.

Lacking wealth or material gifts, I focused on passing down what I had: love, respect, and the lessons of my life. To the grandchildren and great-grandchildren, I could reach, I tried to instill the value of family, kindness, and staying connected. I showed my love not just with words, but with small gestures holding them when they were young, listening when they spoke and praying for their futures.

I hoped they would learn that love does not require money or grand gestures; it is in the time you give, and the care you show.

I also looked like I could teach them respect for others, for themselves, and especially for their elders. Growing up without grandparents, I had learned the value of older, wiser people from neighbors and church members who mentored me. I wanted my grandchildren to honor those around them, to listen to their wisdom and carry it forward. I offered simple advice: *"Treat others as you want to be treated,"* and *"Be honest, even when it's hard."*

These were not current ideas, but they had been the foundation of my life, and I hoped they would guide future generations.

My greatest regret was not being able to give them more materialistic items. Birthdays and Christmases often passed without gifts, as I had many grandchildren and little to share. I worried they might think I did not care, but I did what I could with small gestures, a kind word, or a hug full of love.

My eldest granddaughter, now grown, surprised me once with her memories. She recalled our time together, the moments we shared, and the nickname I gave her. Her words were a gift, proof that the love I had given had taken root, even if I had not seen it then.

Family bonds, to me, are the heartbeat of life. They hold us together, support us when the world feels overwhelming. But I have seen how easily those bonds can weaken today. People are busy, scattered, caught up in their own lives.

Life of an Unknown Lady

My children, grandchildren, and great-grandchildren are no exception; many have drifted apart, and staying connected is harder now. It pains me to see families grow distant, not from lack of love, but because life pulls them in different directions.

I have tried to keep my family close, urging them to call, visit when they can, and remember that family is a gift not everyone has. Growing up without grandparents or extended family, I relied on the kindness of others but always longed for that connection.

I want my descendants to hold onto each other, to support one another in good times and bad times, to know they are never alone.

Legacy, to me, is not about wealth or fame; it is about the good memories you leave behind. I hope my family remembers me as someone who loved them with everything I had, who did her best with what she had. I want them to recall the times I held them as babies, prayed for them as they grew, and cheered for them from my heart.

I hope they carry forward the values I tried to instill love, respect, and resilience. If they are kind to others, lean on faith in tough times, and keep family close, then I will have left a legacy that I taught to all my grandchildren and even my own children.

Conclusion: Well-Lived Life

As I reflect on my life, from humble roots as a small-town girl called Chelock through to who I am today, one thread sparkles the brightest of them all: my love for my family, my faith, and for those who have been kind and compassionate towards me. These strongholds have been my haven in every turbulence, my beacon in times of celebration, and my compass in leading me through life's twists and turns. For me it is a tale of plenty not always in monetary fortune, but in richness in relationships, resilience in fortitude, and faithfulness in allegiance.

My childhood is bathed in warm love from my family. The youngest in my family, I was coddled by my siblings and particularly my brother Willie Smith who arrived from his stint in the army as a holiday themselves. He called me his "little princess," showering candies, cookies, and soda on me and granting my every wish.

My parents also gave themselves freely, their love a security blanket that wrapped around me. That pampering, as exquisite as it was, had lessons I did not understand yet. It made me an indiscipline child who fought against rule and expected things instantly. I learned from those childhood years about love being a gift but in need of balance in order not to impede growth but to encourage it.

As I became a mother, I was adamant about not continuing my childhood patterns. I adored my children deeply, but I fought to treat them fairly, not only showing them love but also teaching them. I wanted them to understand the merit of hard labor, which being resilient was key, and that being strong meant being able to stand on one's own two feet.

Life of an Unknown Lady

It wasn't always easy, times when I wanted to give everything to them, protect them from every trial but I understood that real love meant making them ready for the world, rather than protecting them from it. Seeing them grow into capable, caring adults is a source of pride that surpasses anything in my own life.

One of my proudest times was when I was five years old and read an entire first-grade book from cover to cover before I had even set foot inside a classroom. That instilled in me a love of learning that burned as brightly as anything throughout my elementary years.

I excelled in school plays, basking in the excitement of being in the limelight, my voice booming out onto the stage with poise that overshadowed my years. These experiences were a sample of what I was capable of, a spark that continued even when things in life became complicated. High school was a challenging time, a lapse in confidence, a foolhardy choice to drop out after ninth grade but thinking about that five-year-old girl reading with awestruck eyes reminded me that I was capable of a lot more than my follies.

Life, as I've come to discover, is a mosaic of joy and sorrow, and my struggles have molded me as indelibly as my successes. The loss of my son was an injury that never healed, a sorrow that seeped into my marrow. The loss of my independence as I grew older, living in poverty on limited means, coping day by day in a simple life tested my fortitude.

Through it all, I learned to bend but not break. My older church friends and neighbors, who became surrogates for the grandparents I never had, taught me appreciation. They told me of themselves, of their wisdom, and of themselves being generous in a time of need, demonstrating that in times of dearth, if one looks close enough, one can find plenty. Their teachings became a pillar in my life, a reminder to appreciate what I have in hand, no matter what its seeming lack.

If I were able to sit with my children right now, I would pass on the lessons that have sustained me. I would tell them to fight against spoiling those whom they love deeply, to prize independence earlier, and trust that they are stronger in reality than they realize. I would encourage them to balance in love, give bountifully yet wisely, and that resilience is forged in quiet times of persistence.

To my daughter, I would remind her: "You are a force, able to do more than you can envision. Trust in yourself, even when the world seems heavy." To my son, I would remind him: "Your heart is your strength. Allow it to lead you, but do not permit it to blind you from knowing discipline." These words, I hope, serve as a compass for both of them as they make their way in life.

Lessons of family, resilience, and love have been my beacon of guidance. Family is not just about blood relations, but about people whom you lean on and uplift, no matter how far away. Family is laughter around a humble meal, times of understanding quietly shared, strength in knowing that someone is in your corner and that they believe in you.

Resilience rises from bed in the morning despite feeling drained by grief or emptiness. It is deciding to keep moving forward, finding meaning for what hurts. And love are small things: holding a grandchild's hand, praying for what one child has yet to become, speaking a gentle word to one stranger. These are what make life.

My faith has been my guiding principle, constant through each high and low. It has shown me not only how to pray for what I need but in thanksgiving for what I have.

When despair tore through my life in loss of my son or in the heavy load of life's difficulties, faith was my mooring. It spoke words in my ears reminding me that I am never alone, that there is a plan in my struggles, and that I will survive until my dying breath. Prayer has been my haven, a peaceful dialogue with the divine that roots and blesses me.

As I think about what legacy I hope to leave behind, I pray it is one of kindness and of strength. I would have my family appreciate others, do right even when it is difficult, and live compassionately.

To my children, grandchildren, and great-grandchildren, I would say: Cherish one another. Hold closes those whom you love, treat them kindly, and never take them for granted. Live your best life, be good to each other, and never lose the influence of prayer. These are the things that have kept me strong, and I hope they will keep you strong even after I am no longer around.

To my readers, I give these words of advice: Life is difficult, yet it is beautiful. It will challenge you, shatter you, and piece you together once more. Pray not for what you require, but in thankfulness for what you have. Find strength in those around you, in faith within yourself, and in those little things that make life worth living. A gentle word, a mutually shared laugh, a connection of a moment these are what stitch together a life of substance. Cherish these, and you will discover that even in darkness, light exists.

Life of an Unknown Lady

My own path has had its setbacks. Flunking out of high school was a decision I regretted, a time when impulsiveness beat out wisdom during those impressionable teenage years. But it showed me that setbacks aren't final, they are lessons learned, steppingstones for experience.

I learned through life's tougher school rather than a classroom. Working as a clerk in the general store helped me refine my people skills, regain my confidence, and appreciate the self-worth in being able to make a contribution to my family. The years of hardship, of struggling on little, taught me about grit and appreciation for small victories.

My loss of my son was my greatest challenge. His laughter, his shining eyes, his endless energy were a light to our home. When he was taken from me, it seemed as if the light had gone out of the world. Grief became my shadow; one that I bore step for step. And yet it also showed me the depth of love, the fortitude of memory, and the need to hold on tight to those who are still here. My son's life, though short-lived, was a gift, and one that I pay homage to by living on purpose, by loving him completely, and by sharing his story if people are willing to hear it.

Life of an Unknown Lady

As I grew older, I experienced new challenges, physical limitations, the isolation of an empty nest, the hollow pang of loss of those who had moved on. I discovered new joys as well. My grandchildren restored laughter to my life, their tiny hands pulling on my heartstrings.

My church family became my second family; their encouragement is a reminder that kindness is a resource that never runs out. Throughout it all, I clung to faith, finding comfort in the belief that each trial has a lesson, each joy a blessing.

Now that I stand in autumn of life, I am thankful. To the parents who loved unconditionally, even when I tested them. To brothers and sisters who showered me with love and molded my life in the process. To those children who showed me what love truly is and grandchildren who taught me that life is perpetually new.

To the faith that sustained me in every tempest and the community who helped pick me up when I stumbled. These are the riches of my life, richer than all precious treasures.

I tend to think about the girl I once was Chelock, the inquisitive child who learned to read at five years old, who won people over through her charm, who fell and got up once more. She is still present in my life, her flame unquenched by time.

She teaches me that life is about the journey and not its destination and that each step forward, pleasant or unpleasant as it was, helped shape the woman I became today. I am not flawless, yet I am complete, shaped by love, tested by suffering, and directed by faith.

To my loved ones, I leave these words: You are my heart, my legacy, my reason for living. Be loving, live bravely, and pray in thanksgiving. To the world, I give these words of wisdom: Life is a precious gift that is fragile and ephemeral yet deeply beautiful. Cherish it, hold it close, and never cease to seek out its light. These are the words of a truly well-lived life, and I hope I have succeeded in living one.

www.ingramcontent.com/pod-product-compliance
Lightning Source LLC
Chambersburg PA
CBHW051329120626
46547CB00016B/2461